WOODRUFF
FAMILY LAW GROUP

Essential Guide to Your Family Law Case

Woodruff Family Law Group

PUBLISHER:
Cupcake Buddies, LLC
420 West Market Street
Greensboro, NC 27401

Essential Guide to Your Family Law Case
ISBN: 978-1-940010-20-5

YOU WILL BE OKAY!
YOU WILL SURVIVE THIS!

~

TAKE A DEEP BREATH
AND LET'S BEGIN
THIS JOURNEY TOGETHER.

DEDICATION

This publication is dedicated to those who step forward in emergencies, who take their places on the front lines to help and to protect, who risk their own safety for the benefit of the rest of us. Society's first responders are many and various: law enforcement officers, state troopers, deputies, federal agents, school resource officers, paramedics, emergency medical technicians, firefighters, resource officers, military personnel, sanitation workers. These individuals accept personal risk and the stress associated with it as part of their day-to-day work.

Everyone's work has value, and no one should be taken for granted. But our first responders perform the jobs that most of us cannot do – jobs that most of us would choose not to do. Their jobs are essential for the functioning of our world. Our lives are easier because of them. We owe them more than they owe us. We at Woodruff Family Law Group want them to know that they have our humble, undying gratitude.

THANKS

Thanks to Jessica Bullock, Hannah Smith, Michael Yin, and Carolyn Woodruff for content for this book. Thanks to Marilynn Barr for publication formatting and art work. Thanks to John Davis and Judi Rossabi for final editing.

TABLE OF CONTENTS

CRITICAL TIPS FOR FAMILY LAW

**For more on all these tips,
see the chapter herein dealing with the tip.**

1. Think court filing date for modification. Child Support modification for both child support and spousal support are typically retroactive to the filing date.
2. Think custody modification if any situation with the other parent has created hazards for your child.
3. Follow existing court orders for child custody, or you risk contempt.
4. Be patient. There is Court backlog. Also, be patient in your personal life and avoid Domestic Violence. Take a deep, deep breath.
5. Use the Custody Mediation Office for Child Custody disputes. The Mediation Offices now conduct remote mediations.
6. Consider alternate dispute methods for all issues in your case, such as mediation, arbitration, and collaborative.
7. Don't plan a wedding unless you have your Divorce Judgment in hand.

CHAPTER ONE

CHILD CUSTODY

SECTION ONE

TIPS ON PARENTING THROUGH A CUSTODY CASE

They Never Said Parenting Would Be Easy

By Jessica Bullock, North Carolina Family Law Specialist

Navigating the waters of parenting is not a task for the weak, especially if you find yourself in the middle of a divorce or custody battle. But I'm here to remind you that you can do this. And, if you are in the middle of a divorce or custody battle here in the Triad (or newly separated), having a lawyer that you trust during these times is all that more important.

As a family lawyer and a mom, I have a few tips. Do not be afraid to call your lawyer to ask questions. That's what we're here for. We are here to help guide you through this custody process, especially now. You are not alone.

- Regarding social media, please take a break from it every now and then. It's important to stay up to date on the latest information, but streaming the news 24/7 isn't in anybody's best interest.
- This is a mom tip. Remember to take care of yourself. It is far too easy to get lost in making sure everybody else is okay. Remember, one of the most important things as a parent is to take care of you. That may mean taking 20 minutes to yourself to enjoy a cup of coffee on your porch (or 10 minutes because who am I kidding - the kids will find you) or doing your 15-minute workout in front of the TV. Whatever it is, carve out some time each day to re-energize.
- Create precious memories with your children. Whether it's enjoying a new family hobby like hiking or having a cookout in the backyard, use this extra time when everyone is home together as an opportunity.
- Keep in mind that children are sponges. They take their cues from you, which is another reason to take care of yourself.

- Custody issues can cause a lot of stress and worry over the "what ifs" and over the things you cannot control. One proactive step that you can take is to ensure that you have the legal help needed to navigate these turbulent times.

SECTION TWO

CUSTODY MEDIATION

MEDIATING YOUR CHILD CUSTODY CASE

The North Carolina Custody Mediation program offered through the court system can significantly reduce conflict between parents and serve as the first step in establishing good co-parenting practices. A neutral third party can help parents navigate an emotional time and stay focused on the future in the best interests of their children. Custody cases can easily turn into bitter court battles. Parents who are able to compromise and develop a parenting agreement using this free service usually experience less anxiety and incur fewer legal fees.

Most counties are offering remote orientations and mediations using Zoom, Webex, and other online conferencing programs. The required parenting classes are also offered online. The process of mediation remains the same. The only difference is you won't have to be in the same room as your ex.

Each county is offering its own spin on virtual mediations. Because we practice all over the state, Woodruff Family Law Group receives updates on the latest modifications in several Triad counties. Be sure to check in frequently as technology often changes.

Be sure to stay in contact with your attorney as well. If your mediation is successful, the custody mediator will send a proposed parenting agreement to both parties and their respective counsels. There will be time provided for you to review the proposed agreement and make any changes. It is important that you keep your lawyer up to date on where you are in the mediation process, so they can effectively advocate for you. Find out what remote meeting options they are offering, so when the time comes to review your agreement, you are prepared.

SECTION THREE

WHAT YOU NEED TO KNOW ABOUT YOUR CUSTODY CASE

CHILD CUSTODY

The magic words in North Carolina in child custody trials are "best interest of the child." It is part of the Mission Statement of this Firm to protect the best interests of the children. It is generally best for children if parents agree on a custodial schedule through negotiation and mediation. If no agreement can be reached, after hearing all the evidence, a judge must decide which spouse will make the major decisions affecting the child's life and will provide the child's day-to-day residential supervision.

Except in unusual circumstances, the noncustodial spouse will receive substantial visitation privileges with the child. Rarely is a noncustodial spouse given less than alternate weekends, one-half of the school holidays, and several weeks in the summer. There is no presumptive visitation schedule, and the Court welcomes mutually agreeable visitation settlements.

If you file with the Court for custody in Greensboro or any other court in North Carolina, you are going to have to go to court-ordered mediation with the Court's mediator to discuss how to settle your case in the best interests of the children. You probably are going to have to go to parenting classes as well.

Child custody is an issue that can be raised at any time during the child's minority. Either spouse can petition the Court to change its prior order of custody based on a showing by the moving party that circumstances have changed materially.

GENERAL SUGGESTIONS

Your well-meaning friends may offer you advice about your case. Frequently, such advice is **not accurate,** and you should be cautious in following it. The facts surrounding your marriage, divorce, children, and property are unique; they are different from any other case. Custody proceedings are very **emotional**; the parties sometimes use them to seek revenge. Sometimes one parent will use the children in an attempt to punish the other parent. Prepare your children properly without poisoning their minds about your spouse. Obtain professional advice as necessary. If you need assistance in locating a qualified psychologist or therapist for either yourself or your children, let us know. Continue to cooperate with your spouse where the children's best interests are involved. **Do not** discuss with anyone the confidential matters involved in your case. Friends often pass information to other parties that may get back to your spouse, whether it is intentional or unintentional. It can defeat our efforts to help you.

We strongly suggest that you follow the advice of your attorney or make an initial consultation appointment with this office.

INTERSTATE CUSTODY AND VISITATION

What happens after a custody order is in place, and one of the parents wants to relocate and take the child with them? If the move is merely from Greensboro to Winston-Salem, this may not be that big of an issue, as long as the other parent has the means to travel 30 minutes to see the child and the parents can agree on school selection. However, if the parent decides to move to Texas for a job opportunity, or to be closer to family, this makes things a lot more difficult. A visitation schedule that was made when one parent lived in Greensboro and the other parent lived in High Point is not going to be practical if one of those parents moves to Texas.

The question then becomes, can the parent who is relocating to another state, like Texas, take the child with him or her? North Carolina has developed case law on relocation and what the Court must consider when determining if the relocation necessitates a modification of the custody order. Courts will modify a custody order only if there has been a substantial change in circumstances. Thus, the parent must show a substantial change in circumstances for the Court to even consider the relocation. Only then, when a substantial change in circumstances is shown, will the Court modify the custody order that is currently in place.

"A change in the custodial parent's residence is not itself a substantial change in circumstances affecting the welfare of the child, which justifies a modification of a custody decree." Evans v. Evans, 138 N.C. App. 135 (N.C. App., 2000). Therefore, merely going to the Court and saying that the other parent is moving to Texas, with no other facts focusing on the welfare of the child, will not be enough to get the Court to modify the custody order. Instead, several factors must be considered, all centered on what is in the best interests of the child.

GRANDPARENT RIGHTS

In North Carolina, grandparents have rights under two circumstances:

The first circumstance is if the two natural parents are both unfit (or otherwise cannot take care of a minor child, such as the parent is deceased or seriously disabled). The grandparents have the right to bring the unfit conduct (or the absence of the ability to take care of the child) to the Court's attention and ask that the grandparent be given custody. The Court has to find that the parents have both abrogated their constitutional rights under the Parental Rights Doctrine because of the unfit conduct. The Parental Rights Doctrine is a concept under the U.S. Supreme Court citing parents generally have the paramount natural right to rear their children. The conduct does not have to be serious enough to terminate the parental rights of the parents.

A typical example of unfitness would be drug-addicted parents.

The second area of circumstance arises when the natural parents are in a custody dispute filed with the North Carolina Courts. Perhaps the grandparents are being denied time with their grandchildren.

Under this circumstance, grandparents can file a motion to intervene in the current custody dispute between the natural parents and seek grandparent visitation. Grandparents can file a motion for visitation if:

- There is an ongoing custody case between the natural parents
- The grandparent has a substantial relationship with the child

You might illustrate your substantial relationship with your grandchildren through your beautiful pictures and photo albums.

STEPPARENT OR OTHER THIRD-PARTY RIGHTS

The first question is generally going to be whether the stepparent or other third party has the standing to ask for custodial rights. Standing is a complex legal question and should be discussed thoroughly with your attorney regarding your particular case. The key question will be whether the third party and the child have an established parent-child relationship, and this will be decided on a factual case-by-case basis, as illustrated in the case of Ellison v. Ramos, 130 NC App. 389, 502 W>E>2d 891 (1998).

In *Ellison*, the natural father and the live-in girlfriend companion "parented" the child. The biological mother was medically comatose, so the father was the only biological parent available for parenting. The father and girlfriend broke up, and the girlfriend asked for custody. The trial court dismissed the case because the girlfriend did not have standing. Whoa! The North Carolina Court of Appeals reversed, stating that the trial court had to look at the case on a factual case-by-case basis. The girlfriend's position was that she was the one handling all of the custodial duties for five years. She also alleged that she was the one handling the minor child's specialized medical needs. The Court of Appeals indicated that if a girlfriend could prove she had been the "parent" for five years, the Court could reach the best interests test regarding whether the child could be placed with the girlfriend.

ABUSE AND NEGLECT OF CHILDREN

Like others across the country, Guilford County has its share of child abuse and neglect cases dealt with by experienced family law attorneys. These cases are complex, and the potential outcomes are serious.

North Carolina has specific statutes regarding the abuse and neglect of children, and you need to have an attorney experienced in these matters evaluate your case with you. There are many different elements that lead to a finding that a child is abused or neglected. The complexity of such a finding is a product of the statute, such that having a family law attorney to guide you through the process is critical.

Another factor that makes having an experienced attorney even more valuable is that the stakes are so high. If your case involves the Department of Social Services, you may need representation to protect your parental rights. The Department of Social Services is a powerful agency that can file a petition to strip you of your parental rights and remove your children from your home. This is known as the "death sentence" in a juvenile case, as there is no harsher punishment available in these cases than terminating parental rights. Due to the severe and permanent nature of such an action, having an experienced family law attorney is extremely important.

An order that terminates parental rights essentially means that the parent is no longer legally considered the parent of that juvenile. All of the rights that come along with parental status are stripped away, and the parent is left with absolutely no rights when it comes to that child. This is why termination of parental rights is considered the death sentence of these types of cases.

On the other side of the spectrum, if you believe that a child is being abused or neglected, you have an affirmative duty to report the situation to the Department of Social Services. In most instances, this is and can be done anonymously.

North Carolina law focuses on the best interests of the child. This can be seen both regarding the grounds for termination of parental rights and in the legal duty to report suspected abuse or neglect of a child. At the end of the day, you will likely need help from an experienced family law attorney for the best interests of your child.

CUSTODY & THE DEPARTMENT OF SOCIAL SERVICES

If your case involves the Department of Social Services, you may need representation to protect your parental rights. North Carolina has specific statutes regarding the abuse and neglect of children that are quite tedious and complex. Having an attorney experienced in these matters evaluate your case with you can be extremely helpful. The Department of Social Services is a powerful agency that can file a petition to strip you of your parental rights and remove your children from your home.

The Department of Social Services has established Child Protective Services for juveniles alleged to be abused, neglected, or dependent, which are all technical terms defined in the statute. N.C.G.S. §7B-300 notes that "protective services shall include the screening of reports, the performance of an assessment using either a family assessment response or an investigative assessment response, casework, or other counseling services to parents, guardians, or other caretakers as provided by the director to help the parents, guardians, or other caretakers and the court to prevent abuse or neglect, to improve the quality of childcare, to be more adequate parents, guardians, or caretakers, and to preserve and stabilize family life."

As you can see by the above-quoted statutory language, the Department of Social Services has the authority to take a wide range of actions under the umbrella of Child Protective Services. This authority kicks in as soon as a child is alleged to be abused, neglected, or dependent. Thus, one allegation – maybe from a disgruntled ex-spouse – can get the powerful Department of Social Services involved in your life and your child's life, giving them the authority to take a number of actions without your consent.

According to N.C.G.S. §7B-302(c), "if the assessment indicates that abuse, neglect, or dependency has occurred, the director shall decide whether immediate removal of the juvenile or any other juveniles in the home is necessary for their protection." This means that, following an assessment of the household, the Department of Social Services has the ability to remove the child from the home, if they make the determination that there has been abuse, neglect, or dependency, and removal is needed to protect the child. Therefore, the Department of Social Services has a lot of power over your child once they get involved. Again, the only thing required for their involvement is an allegation of abuse, neglect, or dependency.

Department of Social Services not only has the authority to remove your child from your home, but they also have the power to ask a Judge to terminate your parental rights entirely – provided grounds exist under the statute, and they follow the proper procedure. This demonstrates the power of the Department of Social Services, one of the main reasons why it is a good idea to have an experienced family law attorney at your side throughout the entire process.

Without an experienced attorney, you may have to deal with the involvement of the Department of Social Services longer than necessary, and your child's life may be disrupted to a greater extent than necessary. Our family law attorneys here at Woodruff Family Law Group have the experience to assist you in such matters, along with many other family legal matters.

GUARDIAN AD LITEM

In child custody cases, as well as in child abuse and neglect cases, the Court may appoint a guardian ad litem to represent the best interests of the child. This is in keeping with the much broader emphasis in North Carolina on doing what is determined to be best for the child.

Family law and divorce attorneys here in the Piedmont Triad encounter guardians ad litem in child custody, child abuse, and child neglect cases. Specifically, a guardian ad litem is a fiduciary for your child appointed by the Court generally in one of the following two instances:

1. If there is a Petition filed by the Department of Social Services related to your child, then the Court appoints at State expense a guardian ad litem to be the voice of your child. The guardian will meet with the child and report back to the Court.
2. Sometimes in high conflict custody cases, the Court, generally upon the motion of one of the parents, can appoint a guardian ad litem to be the voice of the child and report to the Court on various issues related to the child. The order to appoint the guardian ad litem in this instance is very important and needs to clearly describe what the guardian should do. The guardian ad litem is generally paid for by one or both parents.

According to N.C.G.S. §7B-601(a), "the duties of the guardian ad litem program shall be to make an investigation to determine the facts, the needs of the juvenile, and the available resources within the family and community to meet those needs; to facilitate, when appropriate, the settlement of disputed issues; to offer evidence and examine witnesses at adjudication; to explore options with the court at the dispositional hearing; to conduct follow-up investigations to ensure that the orders of the court are being properly executed; to report to the court when the needs of the juvenile are not being met; and to protect and promote the best interests of the juvenile until formally relieved of the responsibility by the court."

The duties of the guardian ad litem, as described in the above statute, show the diverse range of issues that a guardian ad litem focuses on, all while keeping in mind what is best for the child. The input of a guardian ad litem in a child custody, child abuse, or child neglect case can be very helpful and useful for the Court to take into consideration. This ensures that there is one specific person whose sole duty is to look after the best interests of the child. This can help to focus the case and make sure that any decisions that are made are done so with the child in mind.

Child abuse cases, child neglect cases, and difficult custody cases are instances where an experienced family law attorney can help guide you through the process to ensure that the outcome is one that considers the impact on the child and is hopefully one in his or her best interests.

"In evaluating the best interests of the child in a proposed relocation, the trial court may appropriately consider several factors including: the advantages of the relocation in terms of its capacity to improve the life of the child; the motives of the custodial parent in seeking the move; the likelihood that the custodial parent will comply with visitation orders when he or she is no longer subject to the jurisdiction of the courts of North Carolina; the integrity of the noncustodial parent in resisting the relocation; and the likelihood that a realistic visitation schedule can be arranged which will preserve and foster the parental relationship with the noncustodial parent." Evans (N.C. App. 2000).

As you can likely see from the quoted case language above, there are many different factors that the Court can consider in determining whether or not to modify the custody order. This gives the Court a lot of discretion in making their determination. However, as mentioned previously, the mere fact of a relocation alone is not enough to justify modifying the custody order; some or all of the factors listed above also have to be analyzed in making such a determination. An experienced family law attorney can assist you in seeking to modify your custody order following a relocation.

SECTION FOUR

ADDITIONAL INFORMATION REGARDING CHILD CUSTODY MATTERS IN NORTH CAROLINA

CHILD CUSTODY BLOG POSTS

Although the magic phrase "best interest of the child" is the guiding light for judicial decisions during a child custody trial, analyzing recent court opinions helps determine circumstances and factors that influence a court's decision. The attorneys at Woodruff Family Law Group have analyzed several court opinions related to child custody in published blog posts. If you would like to read more depth about particular child custody matters that have been before the court, reference Chapter Ten of this book. Additional blog posts can be found at:

North Carolina Divorce Lawyers Blog.
www.northcarolinadivorcelawyersblog.com

CHAPTER TWO

CHILD SUPPORT

SECTION ONE

WHAT YOU SHOULD KNOW ABOUT YOUR CHILD SUPPORT CASE

INFORMATION ON CHILD SUPPORT

The issues of child custody and child support are often linked. The noncustodial spouse will generally be ordered to provide child support by way of periodic payment to the custodial spouse. The Court must follow the North Carolina Child Support Guidelines unless there are factors requiring deviation from the guidelines. The North Carolina Child Support Guidelines can be found here:

North Carolina Child Support Guidelines.
www.ncdhhs.gov/divisions/social-services/child-support-services/nc-child-support-centralized-collections

If there are reasons for deviation such as special needs of a child or high income in the family, then the determination is based, in part, on financial statements prepared by the custodial spouse. These financial statements will be filed with the Court. The Court will then review the financial statements itemizing the incomes and expenses of each spouse.

It should be noted that a noncustodial spouse's child support obligation continues until the child reaches the age of 18 or finishes high school (whichever occurs last). However, if the child is otherwise emancipated, payment shall terminate at that time. A party by agreement may obligate himself or herself to make such payments beyond these time limits.

Both child custody and child support are issues that can be raised at any time during the child's minority. Either spouse can petition the Court to change its prior order of custody or support based on a showing by the moving party that circumstances have changed materially.

CHILD SUPPORT CENTRAL COLLECTIONS

North Carolina Child Support Central Collections has the address of P.O. Box 90006, Raleigh, North Carolina 27675. The website is

North Carolina Child Support Central Collections.
www.ncdhhs.gov/divisions/social-services/child-support-services/nc-child-support-centralized-collections

A check or money order is made out to N.C. Child Support and mailed to Centralized Collections with a payment coupon in the self-addressed envelope provided by Centralized Collections.

TAX ISSUES RELATED TO CHILDREN

- Child support is not taxable as income to the payee spouse.
- Child support is not a deduction to the payor spouse.
- Unless there is an agreement to the contrary, the primary custodial spouse gets the child's tax exemption.
- You may be eligible for head of household if you are the custodial parent.
- You may be eligible for childcare credits even if you do not have the child's exemption.

LOOKING AHEAD: MINIMUM WAGE AND CHILD SUPPORT

The North Carolina Child Support Guidelines state that the guidelines should be reviewed periodically (at least once every three years). However, this does not preclude the guidelines from being reviewed prior to the three-year mark. The next re-writing for the current North Carolina Child Support Guidelines should occur in 2022, when an economist will look at inflationary effects on the child support amounts. However, we may see a review of the guidelines prior to 2022 if the Federal Minimum Wage changes to $15.00 an hour.

The guidelines calculate a parent's child support obligation based upon his or her actual gross income from any source. The guidelines also allow for potential or imputed income to be assigned to a parent if the parent has no recent work history or vocational training. However, the current guidelines stipulate that potential income should not be less than the minimum hourly wage for a 35-hour workweek. A jump from the current minimum wage of $7.25 an hour in North Carolina to $15.00 an hour can significantly impact child support calculations, as one can imagine.

The ripple effects of a change to the Federal Minimum Wage are yet to be seen—if seen at all. However, it will be interesting to see how the guidelines are reviewed and amended as a result of such monumental changes within the workforce.

SECTION TWO

ADDITIONAL INFORMATION REGARDING CHILD SUPPORT MATTERS IN NORTH CAROLINA

CHILD SUPPORT BLOG POSTS

As previously stated, several factors can result in the court deviating from the North Carolina Child Support Guidelines to determine the appropriate child support obligation for either parent. The attorneys at Woodruff Family Law Group have analyzed several court opinions related to child support in published blog posts. If you would like to read more in depth about particular child support matters that have been before the court, reference Chapter Ten of this book. Additional blog posts can be found at:

North Carolina Divorce Lawyers Blog.
www.northcarolinadivorcelawyersblog.com

CHAPTER THREE

SPOUSAL SUPPORT

SECTION ONE

POST SEPARATION SUPPORT

POST SEPARATION SUPPORT

North Carolina no longer has temporary Alimony but has changed the terminology to Post Separation Support. The court is instructed to award Post Separation Support based upon the following:

- Financial needs of the parties;
- Accustomed standard of living;
- Present employment income and other recurring earnings of each party from any source;
- Earning abilities of both spouses;
- Separate and marital debt service obligations;
- Necessary living expenses of both parties;
- Each person's respective legal obligations to support any other person;
- Pre-separation *marital misconduct* of both parties.

Post Separation Support is recoverable in North Carolina *only* to the dependent spouse and *only* paid by the supporting spouse.

Marital Misconduct means any of the following acts that occur during the marriage and prior to or on the date of separation:

- Illicit sexual behavior, which includes acts of sexual or deviant sexual intercourse, deviant sexual acts, or sexual acts voluntarily engaged in with someone other than the other spouse;
- Causing an involuntary separation in consequence of a criminal act;
- Abandoning the other spouse; Maliciously turning the other spouse out of doors;
- Cruel and barbarous treatment endangering the life of the other spouse;
- Indignities rendering the condition of the other spouse intolerable and life burdensome;

- Reckless spending of the income of either party or the destruction, waste, diversion or concealment of assets;
- Excessive use of alcohol or drugs so as to render the condition of the other spouse intolerable and life burdensome;
- Willful failure to provide necessary subsistence according to one's means and condition so as to render the condition of the other spouse intolerable and life burdensome.

For more on marital misconduct, see our blog posts:

Alimony and Marital Misconduct
www.northcarolinadivorcelawyersblog.com/alimony-and-marital-misconduct/

Limits on Alimony as a Result of Condoned Marital Misconduct
www.northcarolinadivorcelawyersblog.com/limits-on-alimony-as-a-result-of-condoned-marital-misconduct/

SECTION TWO

ALIMONY

ALIMONY

ENTITLEMENT TO ALIMONY

You must be the **dependent spouse,** which means you are actually substantially dependent upon the other spouse for support or substantially in need of support from the other spouse. It must be **equitable** to award the dependent spouse Alimony. Equitable is determined on the following relevant factors:

- Financial needs of the parties;
- Accustomed standard of living;
- Present employment income and other recurring earnings of each party from any source;
- Earning abilities of both spouses;
- Separate and marital debt service obligations;
- Living expenses of both parties necessary for the support of both;
- Each party's respective legal obligations to support any other person.
- Finally, illicit sexual behavior plays a determinative role in entitlement to permanent Alimony.

If you are the dependent spouse and you engaged in uncondoned illicit sexual behavior during the marriage and prior to the date of separation, you will not be entitled to Alimony unless the supporting spouse also participated in an act of uncondoned illicit sexual behavior during the marriage prior to the date of separation.

If you are the supporting spouse, your spouse shall be entitled to Alimony if you engaged in an uncondoned illicit sexual act during the marriage prior to the date of separation (and the dependent spouse is not guilty of the same conduct).

If both spouses have engaged in an uncondoned illicit sexual act, then Alimony may be denied or awarded in the discretion of the court after consideration of all the other circumstances.

AMOUNT AND DURATION OF PERMANENT ALIMONY

Who decides? The trial court decides in its discretion the amount, duration, and manner of payment of Alimony. What are the **relevant factors** the court must consider in determining the manner, amount, and duration of payment of permanent Alimony?
N.C.G.S. 50-16.3A(b):

1. The marital misconduct of either of the spouses, which may be determined by a jury (see marital misconduct under Post Separation Support as these factors are the same);
2. The relative earnings and earning capacities of the spouses;
3. The ages and the physical, mental and emotional conditions of the spouses;
4. The amount and source of earned and unearned income of both spouses, including but not limited to earnings, dividends, and benefits such as medical, retirement, insurance, social security or others;
5. The duration of the marriage;
6. The contribution by one spouse to the education, training or increased earning power of the other spouse;
7. The extent to which the earning power, expenses or financial obligations of a spouse will be affected by reason of serving as the custodian of a minor child;
8. The standard of living of the spouses established during the marriage;
9. The relative education of the spouses and the time necessary to acquire sufficient education or training to enable the spouse seeking Alimony to find employment to meet his or her reasonable economic needs;

10. The relative assets and liabilities of the spouses and the relative debt service;
11. requirements of the spouses, including legal obligations of support;
12. The property brought to the marriage by either spouse;
13. The contribution of a spouse as a homemaker;
14. The relative needs of the spouses;
15. The Federal and State tax ramifications of the Alimony award;
16. Any other factors relating to the economic circumstances of the parties that the court finds to be just and proper.

MODIFICATION/TERMINATION OF ALIMONY AND/OR POST SEPARATION SUPPORT

Alimony or Post Separation Support can be modified or terminated by the court upon a showing of changed circumstances. Alimony or Post Separation Support terminates: upon the death of either party, upon the remarriage of the recipient spouse, and/or upon the cohabitation of the recipient spouse.

What is cohabitation? The act of two adults dwelling together continuously and habitually in a private heterosexual or homosexual relationship. Evidence includes: the **voluntary mutual assumption of those marital rights, duties, and obligations which are usually manifested by married people and which include, but are not necessarily dependent on, sexual relations.**

PROCEDURAL TIMING: ALIMONY AND POST SEPARATION SUPPORT

Your case for Alimony or Post Separation Support must be pending in the court prior to your absolute divorce. The divorce, however, does not terminate the Alimony or Post Separation award already in place automatically. The claim for Alimony may be heard on the merits prior to the entry of a judgment for Equitable Distribution, and, if awarded, the issues of the amount and of whether a spouse is a dependent or supporting spouse may be reviewed by the court after the conclusion of the equitable distribution claim.

NEW RULES ON TAX DEDUCTIONS FOR ALIMONY

The Tax Cut and Jobs Act of 2017 included a change to how Alimony would be taxed at the Federal level. For divorces finalized after 2018, Alimony is no longer deductible for the payor and no longer considered taxable income for the recipient. Carolyn Woodruff is a Certified Public Accountant who can advise on the tax ramifications of all issues that arise from separation and divorce, and is ready to assist you on these matters.

FOR MORE INSIGHT ON ALIMONY, SEE OUR BLOG!

Limits on Alimony as a Result of Marital Misconduct

www.northcarolinadivorcelawyersblog.com/limits-on-alimony-as-a-result-of-condoned-marital-misconduct/

Goodbye Alimony? Not So Fast!

www.northcarolinadivorcelawyersblog.com/goodbye-alimony-not-so-fast/

CHAPTER FOUR

EQUITABLE DISTRIBUTION

SECTION ONE

EQUITABLE DISTRIBUTION

Your equitable distribution claim MUST be pending in the Court prior to your divorce. Of course, you can settle at any time prior to the divorce with a Property Settlement Agreement.

EQUITABLE DISTRIBUTION

PROPERTY DIVISION & PROPERTY SETTLEMENT AGREEMENTS

If you and your estranged agree on a property division, a team member at Woodruff Family Law Group can prepare an appropriate and legally binding, notarized Property Settlement Agreement. We caution against generic forms from the internet as these do not necessarily protect your rights are not unique to your situation.

Rule One: Never get your Absolute Divorce unless all Property and Spousal Support rights are either settled or appropriately pending before the Court. You are FOREVER barred from bringing a Property or Spousal Support claim after the Absolute Divorce is final.

There are avenues to settling a property division case without going to court. You and your team members at Woodruff Family Law Group will look at an alternative to finishing your case without the help of the Court - if finishing your case is your objective. There are options for Mediation, Collaborative Law, and Arbitration available as Alternative Dispute Resolution. Go to our website at

Woodruff Family Law Group.
www.woodrufflawfirm.com

Click on the Services tab. There you will find more information on Mediation, Arbitration, and Collaborative Law.

EQUITABLE DISTRIBUTION & THE COURT

The Court (unless settled by agreement, which can be done at any time after you separate) will divide the property owned by you and your spouse. You must have a claim for equitable distribution pending on the date of absolute divorce, or your rights are gone. In North Carolina, this process is described as "Equitable Distribution of Marital Assets."

There are three types of property that must be considered.

- "Separate property" includes all property owned by either spouse before the marriage, property acquired during the marriage by one spouse by inheritance or gift from a third party, and property acquired after the date of separation with post-separation earnings. A gift from one spouse to the other during the marriage is marital property unless the donor states at the time of the conveyance that it is intended to be separate property.
- "Marital Property" includes property presently owned that was acquired during the marriage except property determined to be "separate property." "Marital property" includes all vested pension and retirement benefits acquired during the marriage and prior to separation.
- "Divisible property" is property subject to equitable distribution upon divorce and is defined as real and personal property that includes the appreciation and diminution in value of the marital property and other divisible property acquired as a result of actions of the parties during the marriage but before separation; passive income from marital property received after separation; and increases in marital debt including finance charges and interest related to marital debt.

The law further creates a presumption that an in-kind distribution of marital or divisible property is equitable but allows this presumption to be rebutted by the greater weight of the evidence, or by evidence that the property is a closely held business entity or is otherwise not susceptible of division in-kind. The new law makes it easier for the Court to make interim distributions of the property prior to the final judgment. Under current law, before an interim distribution may be made, the spouse must show good cause for such a distribution. The new law authorizes the Court to make interim distributions unless good cause is shown that such a distribution should not be made.

The new law further provides that evidence of pre-separation and post-separation value is competent as corroborative evidence of the value of the marital property as of the date of separation. Divisible property and divisible debt are valued as of the date of distribution.

The change relating to motions for interim allocation applies to motions for interim allocation filed after October 1, 1997. The remainder of the new law herein above applies to actions for equitable distribution filed on or after that date.

There are statutory factors the Court must consider in deciding whether an equal division is appropriate in your case. These factors are:

- Income, property, and debts of a party;
- Support obligations from prior marriages;
- Length of marriage and age and health of each party;
- Needs of the custodial spouse to own or to possess the marital homeplace and household effects;
- The expectation of retirement benefits which are separate property;
- Efforts made by each spouse to acquire property;
- Contributions of one spouse to the education of the other;
- Direct contributions that increase the value of separate property;
- Liquid or non-liquid nature of property;
- Difficulty in valuing interest in a business;
- Tax consequences;
- Actions taken by either party to preserve or waste marital assets; and
- Other factors.

Adultery is NOT considered in the settlement of property rights.

EQUITABLE DISTRIBUTION INVENTORY AFFIDAVIT

If your equitable distribution case goes to litigation (i.e., a Complaint is filed), then the first party to file the equitable distribution claim must serve an inventory on the opposing side. The opposing side has 30 days to file a responsive inventory affidavit. The affidavit must:

- List items of marital property
- List items of separate property
- Give the estimated date of separation value

N.C.G.S. 50-21 specifically provides: that these affidavits shall be subject to amendment and "shall not be binding at trial as to completeness or value."

CHANGES WITH REGARD TO INVENTORY AFFIDAVITS

Willful obstruction or delay can subject you to severe financial penalties and can cause the Court to not allow you to present your side of the case.

On the Inventory Affidavit, you have to make a full and fair disclosure of the assets you own on the date of separation. Without such a disclosure of the assets and liabilities, the court will not be able to accurately divide the property equitably. You would want your spouse to make a full disclosure of their assets, especially any that you do not have access to, so you should do the same in order to make the process as straightforward as possible. If you have reason to believe your spouse is withholding or hiding assets on their Affidavit, consult with your Family Law Specialist to find out how we can reveal those assets.

After your absolute divorce, the Court (unless settled by agreement, which can be done at any time after you separate) will divide the property owned by you and your spouse. YOU MUST HAVE A CLAIM FOR EQUITABLE DISTRIBUTION PENDING ON THE DATE OF DIVORCE,

OR YOUR RIGHTS ARE GONE. In North Carolina, this process is described as "Equitable Distribution of Marital Assets."

There are two types of property that must be considered. "Separate property" includes all property owned by either spouse before the marriage, property acquired during the marriage by one spouse by inheritance or gift from a third party, and property acquired after the date of separation with post-separation earnings. A gift from one spouse to the other during the marriage is marital property unless the donor states at the time of the conveyance that it is intended to be separate property. "Marital Property" includes property presently owned that was acquired during the marriage except property determined to be "separate property."

"Marital property" includes all vested pension and retirement benefits. As you might imagine, the law of equitable distribution is extremely complex; this brief description is a gross over-simplification. Please discuss the specifics of your case with your lawyer in our firm.

Separate property will be kept by the spouse who owns it while marital property will be divided between the parties by the Court. While there is not a precise formula for dividing property, there is a strong tendency in North Carolina to divide the property or its equivalent value equally.

Marital misconduct, such as adultery, is NOT considered in the property settlement or property rights. (Marital misconduct is considered with regard to Alimony.)

TAXATION OF PROPERTY SETTLEMENTS

Generally, a division of marital property is a nontaxable event. (Discuss exceptions with your attorney.) Generally, if property is transferred between spouses pursuant to an agreement or court order, it will neither be taxed as income nor allowed as a deduction. There may be tax consequences, however, when funds are transferred from a retirement plan and Individual Retirement Accounts and when marital assets are sold to third parties. There are also traps that need to be evaluated with regard to your specific case.

SECTION TWO

QUALIFIED DOMESTIC RELATIONS ORDERS

Be patient with the qualification process.
Plan administrators must "qualify" the Domestic Relations Order.

UNDERSTANDING THE QDRO/IRA PROCESS

This information introduces you to the Qualified Domestic Relations Orders (QDROs) process. The QDRO process can be a time-consuming ordeal requiring numerous drafts of the Domestic Relations Order (D.R.O.) to be acceptable to the Plan Administrator.

WHAT IS A QDRO?

A Qualified Domestic Relations Order, or QDRO, is a Court order that has been Qualified by the Plan Administrator. QDRO is used to divide qualified retirement plan assets in a divorce with no tax consequences to the parties involved. I.R.A.s do not use D.R.O. or QDRO. I.R.A.s may only require forms supplied by the investment brokerage house.

THE QDRO PROCESS/I.R.A. PROCESS

After completing your property settlement via either Agreement or Order, a D.R.O. or other domestic relations Order or IRA order/forms will be drafted according to the provisions stated in your property settlement agreement or Court Order and consistent with the requirements of a Plan or brokerage house (such as Fidelity).

To properly draft the D.R.O. or other domestic relations order, information needs to be provided to the drafting attorney. The information required includes, but is not necessarily limited to, the latest account statement and any "model QDRO language" provided by the Plan.

Every Plan is different, and each Plan requires specific language that meets the specifications of that particular Plan Administrator. "Model QDRO language" can be beneficial. Different Plan Administrators can interpret identical D.R.O. provisions in different ways. For example, a D.R.O. that may be acceptable to Merrill Lynch may not be acceptable to Fidelity.

We sometimes send domestic relations orders to the Plan Administrator for Pre-Approval before having you sign the D.R.O. In the pre-approval process, the Plan Administrator reviews the proposed D.R.O. to determine whether it will be acceptable as a valid QDRO or whether the Plan will require revisions before qualifying the Order. The pre-approval process can take the reviewer anywhere from a couple of weeks to several months to complete. Please note that it is not unusual for the Plan Administrator to reject the first and occasionally second drafts submitted to them. Not all Plan Administrators will pre-approve; there are other reasons not to seek pre-approval as well.

After receiving the pre-approval of the D.R.O., the Order is ready to be executed. Upon the signatures of all the parties and the presiding Judge and entry by the Court, a certified copy is sent to the Plan Administrator. Upon submission of the certified copy of the D.R.O. to the Plan Administrator, the Plan Administrator has up to 180 days under federal law to determine whether the Order should be "qualified." This time may be shortened when the Order is submitted with the pre-approval letter.

Once the Order is qualified as a QDRO, the Plan Administrator will probably segregate the amount designated in the QDRO into a separate account for the Alternate Payee (person receiving the funds).

To avoid taxation on the awarded money, the alternate payee must transfer the funds into an appropriate IRA account in a custodian-to-custodian transfer. The alternate payee will be responsible for any taxes, including early withdrawal penalties, when the funds are withdrawn from the account. There are special rules in 401(k) Plans for taking a withdrawal without penalties, which you can discuss with your attorney if you are interested.

2019 AMENDMENTS TO EQUITABLE DISTRIBUTION OF PENSIONS, RETIREMENT ACCOUNTS, AND DEFERRED COMPENSATION.

A new law passed in 2019 made revisions to the rules governing classification, valuation, and distribution of pensions, retirement accounts, and deferred compensation benefits. One main goal of the amendment was to clarify that deferred compensation may take many forms, not just those similar to retirement plans (such as a 401(K). Another goal was to provide a separate cause of action (or a motion) that would allow a Court to issue an Order to distribute these types of assets, regardless of whether a claim for Equitable Distriubtion was filed. The other major changes are complex, and should your case require it, our Family Law Specialists have already adapted to the changes and are ready to advise regarding retirement.

FOR MORE ON EQUITABLE DISTRIBUTION AND QDROS, SEE OUR BLOG!

When Stock Options Are Not Stock Options
www.northcarolinadivorcelawyersblog.com/when-stock-options-are-not-stock-options/

Inheritance and Equitable Distribution
www.northcarolinadivorcelawyersblog.com/inheritance-and-equitable-distribution/

Business Goodwill and the Effect on Value
www.northcarolinadivorcelawyersblog.com/business-goodwill-and-the-effect-on-value/

CHAPTER FIVE

DIVORCE

SECTION ONE

GENERAL DIVORCE INFORMATION

ABSOLUTE DIVORCE

In North Carolina, absolute divorces are almost always obtained on the basis of one year's separation. After you and your spouse have lived separate continuously for one year, without resuming the marital relationship, either of you may obtain an absolute divorce. Attempts at reconciliation marked by isolated instances of sexual intercourse will not automatically end the period of continuous separation. However, instances of sexual intercourse and nights spent together may add to the totality of circumstances sufficient to cause a court to find that you have renewed the marital relationship voluntarily. Should a court so find, the twelve-month clock will be reset. You cannot file for an absolute divorce until the next business day after your one-year separation. For example, if you and your spouse separated on February 12, 2020, you cannot file for your absolute divorce until February 13, 2021. Then your spouse is served with a Summons and Complaint. From the point of service, your spouse has 30 days in which to answer your Complaint and may even get a 30-day extension to answer your Complaint, making it 60 days before you can get a court date. If your spouse does not choose to answer your Complaint, which he/she can do, we can file automatically for a court date after the 30-day answer period has lapsed. It takes at least three weeks to get a court day in Guilford County (each county is different) from the time the 30-day answer period has lapsed, or we receive an answer, thus making it at least seven to eight weeks before you actually obtain your absolute divorce.

NEVER PLAN A NEW WEDDING DATE
OR THE PURCHASE OF A NEW HOME
(unless you are a "free trader")
UNTIL YOU HAVE YOUR DIVORCE JUDGMENT IN HAND!

CHANGE OF NAME

The female spouse may wish to resume her maiden name as part of the divorce decree. We can accomplish this easily at no additional charge. If you want that service, let us know before we prepare the absolute divorce complaint or answer a lawsuit. There is no provision under the law for a male spouse to force his wife to resume the use of her maiden name.

ACCOMMODATING NEW RELATIONSHIPS

You are married until the divorce is granted. Post-separation pre-divorce dating can be used by your spouse against you and your new partner. Common problems are as follows:

- Your partner may be sued for alienation of affection or criminal conversation;
- With regard to Alimony and Post Separation Support, post-date-of-separation marital misconduct may be used as corroborating evidence that misconduct occurred during the marriage and prior to the date of separation.

If these are risks you are prepared to take, make sure you tell your attorney about all such actions on your part so that they can be prepared to respond to these circumstances.

BEWARE! DOMESTIC VIOLENCE TIPS

Domestic Violence Laws Are Strong in This State!

- Do not touch your ex (estranged) spouse for any reason. (Assault)
- Do not go inside the residence of your ex (estranged) spouse, even if your name is on the deed, and it used to be your home. (Trespass)

- Do not telephone your ex (estranged) spouse excessively. (Harassment)
- Do not telephone the lover of your ex (estranged) spouse. (Harassment)
- Do not follow, either in your vehicle or on foot, your ex (estranged) spouse. (Stalking)
- Do not go to the place of business of your ex (estranged) spouse. (Harassment)
- Do not email or write your ex (estranged) spouse. (Harassment)
- Do not block the path of your ex (estranged) spouse to a doorway or car. (False imprisonment)
- Do not use corporal punishment on your children unless both parents clearly agree. (Assault, DSS)
- Do not confront your ex (estranged) spouse concerning fault issues, such as adultery, alcohol abuse, drug abuse, etc. Let your attorney do this in the legal process. (Harassment)
- Do not use curse words either around or concerning your ex (estranged) spouse. (Harassment)
- Do not threaten to kill your ex (estranged) spouse, EVEN AS A JOKE. (Attempted Murder)
- Do not throw anything (even a paperclip) at your ex (estranged) spouse. (Assault)
- Do not remove a child from the arms or car of your ex (estranged) spouse. (Assault)

CHAPTER SIX

DEALING WITH THE COURTS & ALTERNATIVE DISPUTE RESOLUTION

COVID-19 HAS SLOWED THE COURTS, NOW WHAT?

If you have a family law case pending in any county in the Piedmont Triad, your case is likely going to be slowed down in the court system due to the closures caused by COVID-19. Our courts have closed multiple times due to positive cases of COVID-19. During those closures, the courts are only hearing limited family law issues, which include matters such as temporary restraining orders, domestic violence, and emergency custody. Even when open, Courts have had to limit the amount of cases to ensure public safety. This has pushed back many non-emergency cases, and new ones are being filed daily. The Court will take some time to catch up.

Do you have to sit around and wait months and months for a hearing? Not necessarily! There are several options available. Your divorce lawyer can tell if one of these options is appropriate for your case.

MEDIATION

The first option is mediation, where the parties and their attorneys hire a third-party neutral mediator to attempt to resolve the issues in your case. Currently, mediations are mostly being held remotely through video conferencing software such as Webex. In most cases, NC Statutes require that equitable distribution, alimony, and custody be mediated prior to hearings; therefore, this is a great opportunity to complete required mediation if you are able.

ARBITRATION

Have you tried mediation and it was unsuccessful? Another option is arbitration, which is set up like a court hearing, with an arbitrator (who is a family lawyer) serving as your Judge. Testimony, witnesses, and exhibits are presented just as you would in court, and the Arbitrator issues a ruling as a Judge would. Your arbitration award is then confirmed by the Courts as a court order. This can be a very effective tool to have your matter heard and completed efficiently. Woodruff Family Law Group has experience navigating the arbitration process. Talk with your lawyer to see if this option is appropriate for your case.

REMOTE COURT HEARINGS

Remote court hearings are an option in certain matters in certain counties. Guilford County has issued a set of guidelines to determine which matters are eligible to be heard through remote channels. Guilford County courts are hearing matters such as post-separation support, temporary custody, and child support, as well as certain discovery and other legal argument motions. They are time-limited, and you are also limited on the number of exhibits you may present; however, these online hearings can serve as a valuable tool to keep your case going. But not all counties operate with the same remote guidelines. Please visit the COVID-19 tab on our website to read more about each county's set of guidelines.

While these times may be extremely frustrating if you need the court's assistance, please talk with your attorney to determine if there are ways to move your case forward in the interim. We are here to help!

CHAPTER SEVEN

HIRING THE RIGHT ATTORNEY

SECTION ONE

ABOUT US

WOODRUFF FAMILY LAW GROUP MISSION STATEMENT

Through care, integrity, and honesty, Woodruff Family Law Group works to provide creative and impactful solutions for our clients. We seek each client's most important goals and objectives. From the initial consultation and throughout every step we take together in the legal process, each client and every member of their family is of the utmost importance to us. With this approach, every client can be on the road to a promising divorce recovery and a bright future.

We are open and offering consultations.
Call us at 336-272-9122 to schedule today.
Ask for the Initial Consultation Team.

Here are some examples of
What Our Clients Have to Say.
Visit
Woodruff Family Law Group Reviews
www.woodrufflawfirm.com/reviews.html
for more feedback from our clients!

** Pursuant to the Rules of Professional Responsibility, the results of all clients under their specific facts may differ from your results under the facts of your case.*

"I would like to thank attorney Jonathan Csuka for handling my case. Jon handled a case for me that no other attorney has been able to do in 14 years. It was handled and closed in less than 6 months. He is a true professional and is extremely knowledgeable and intelligent with what he does. On a scale of 1 to 10, I would give him a 10+. Highly recommended."

M.B., February 11, 2020

~

"Very informative and easy to talk to."

Anonymous Initial Consult, February 2, 2020

~

"Jessica was great. She answered several questions and really understood my objectives for my separation."

A.V., November 7, 2019

~

"We felt very comfortable with Ms. Clay and have complete confidence in her as she led us forward."

D.C., November 5, 2019

~

"Adam Furr listened to me, gave me good advice, and was down to Earth. He didn't judge me or talk down to me, and he didn't rush me. He was very helpful, and I have some things to consider now. Thank you."

Anonymous Initial Consult, October 10, 2019

~

"I felt comfortable meeting Jessica S. Bullock and feel that she will fight for me."

L.R., September 28, 2019

~

"Adam, Hannah & Gull have been very helpful with my many breakdowns and questions. They are very professional but also they care about me and what I am going through, and that means a lot."

R.H., September 10, 2019

~

"I was made to feel very comfortable during a very stressful conversation. Very professional!"

Anonymous Initial Consult, August 21, 2019

~

"I liked hearing very practical advice. Everything was easy to understand."

Anonymous Initial Consult, August 9, 2019

~

"Everyone I have spoken to or dealt with at this agency (all levels and positions) has always been professional as well as kind, pleasant, personal, and thoughtful. After professional, there are not many qualities a person could hope to expect from a few individuals working in a law office much less from every individual dealt with in one law group."

R.A., June 26, 2019

~

"My consultation was handled with a professionalism beyond my expectation. I felt comfortable talking with my attorney with complete detail. Everyone in the office from the entrance to private meeting rooms was courteous and informative, answering all my questions."

J.W., June 5, 2019

~

"Extremely pleased with the urgency I feel Carolyn have shown towards my case."

S.T., April 15, 2019

~

"From the moment I met Carolyn Woodruff, I knew that I had someone on my side who would work hard to meet the needs within my case. I was not prepared for the road ahead, but with her guidance, I was able to get through it. She and her team were prompt to respond to my inquiries, and I never felt like I could not ask questions or give input. She is very thorough, and she knows just what questions to ask to delve deep into an issue until she is able to come upon a concrete answer. I was extremely impressed with her financial knowledge, which was most helpful for my case. She's a real fighter, and she never backs down until she knows we've reached a satisfying outcome. The firm, as a whole, was friendly and calm, and the staff always did what they could to make me feel comfortable in a situation that was not comfortable. In particular, Steve Coggin was extremely helpful with the financial aspects of my case, and he was able to explain things to me in an easy manner. He was kind and responsive to any questions I had. Like Carolyn, he kept digging into my case for all the information needed to give us a good resolution. Overall, I was extremely happy with my experience. If I need additional help with my case in the future, I will always feel comfortable and welcome by the firm."

K.A., March 18, 2019

~

"I give Adam Furr five out of five stars. My custody case had some out of the ordinary circumstances, and despite that, he was able to help me. He never felt hard to talk to, and I was surprised to receive updates from him after hours some days. He even checked in on my situation while he was on vacation. He took special care with my case and was able to give us the edge we needed against the other side. The staff and firm were always welcoming and polite. While my experience with the support staff was limited, Amy Setzer and Meghan Driscoll were always quick to help me. While I hope to never need their services again, I would highly recommend Adam and the firm to anyone needing assistance in a family law case. I cannot thank them enough for what they have done for me."

W.F., February 20, 2019

SECTION TWO

WHY HIRE US?

WE'RE COMPETENT

"Fighting for Justice in Your Family Law Case."

When you hire us, you hire our TEAM. Among our eight top-rated attorneys, you'll have over 60 years of cumulative Family Law experience at your side. You'll have five Family Law Specialists (few attorneys in the state have earned this credential), four N.C. Bar Certified Paralegals, a CPA, and a Certified Valuation Analyst (business valuator). You'll have a diverse support staff of highly qualified, professional legal assistants proficient in a broad range of fields, including accounting, human services, administration, and business.

When it comes to Divorce & Separation, Child Custody & Support, and Equitable Distribution & Property Division, the TEAM at Woodruff is capable of handling the most complex matters. We can efficiently handle simple matters as well. Added to that is the ability to offer complete financial analysis and accurate valuation of businesses, pensions, and other assets. The combination means that with TEAM Woodruff Family Law Group behind you, you'll have an edge.

Because the law isn't the only thing we know.
At Woodruff Family Law Group, we know what we're doing.

WE'RE COMPASSIONATE

"You Matter. Your Family Matters."

When you hire us, you'll see that at Woodruff Family Law Group, we get it. Circumstances have you anxious. Worrying about the well-being of your family - your marriage, your children, your future - is stressful and scary. This isn't just a 'problem' to be resolved. It's your life. Legal advice is not the only thing you need right now; you deserve support, empathy, and understanding too. Family Law is our concentration. That experience makes us sensitive to the emotional journey our clients are about to face.

That's why in addition to lending our expertise, we strive to ensure the people we work with understand they're more than just a number to us.

When you're a client here, we'll smile and greet you by name, because we'll recognize you. We'll ask how you're doing because we genuinely care. You'll grab a bottle of water from the fridge, or we'll bring you a cup of coffee because we want you to feel comfortable and welcomed, and you'll camp out in a conference room while you wait for court because we don't want you to feel alone.

Those services aren't fringe benefits. They represent our effort to show the clients in our family that we see them. We pride ourselves on continuously pursuing more of the 'little things' because it makes what they're going through a little less hard.

We do more than help our clients 'get done.'
At Woodruff Family Law Group, we help our clients 'get through.'

WE'RE COMMITTED

"Individualized Strategies Tailored to Your Particular Law Needs."

When you hire us, we'll walk with you the whole way. We have a devoted team of attorneys and staff pledged to a firm that concentrates exclusively on Family Law. This is a scary time for you. Your family is in jeopardy; you aren't sure what to do next. That's where we come in.

From your initial consult to the conclusion of your case, we engage in dialogue and keep you informed of what's happening—what to expect—step-by-step. We listen to your needs and work side-by-side with you to develop a personalized plan to achieve those objectives. The knowledgeable and visionary lawyers at Woodruff Family Law Group will navigate you through this complicated process. We pride ourselves on our fairness, integrity, and our dedication to fiercely advocating for each client's needs because their happiness and peace are our success.

We don't work on jobs.
At Woodruff Family Law Group, we work with people.

WE'RE CREATIVE

"Outside-of-the-box solutions for inside-of-the-house problems."

When you hire us, we'll consider not just the facts surrounding your situation, but the personalities, the emotions, and all the nuances in between. To us, this isn't just a case—it's your case, and it's unlike any other.

Our office is a composite of diverse perspectives, backgrounds, and skills. The Woodruff TEAM works in an atmosphere of harmony and trust that provides a positive self-image for each member. From the newest legal assistant to Carolyn Woodruff herself, the ideas, strengths, and contributions of each employee are valued equally. The culture of our firm has created a cohesive unit of efficient, passionate individuals who feel 100% invested in every client we help.

The collaboration of expertise, abilities, and resources enable us to customize innovative solutions that meet the best interests of every unique and valued individual who walks through our door.

We don't work on problems.
At Woodruff Family Law Group,
we work on solutions.

WE *ARE* WOODRUFF FAMILY LAW GROUP

WHY HIRE US?

Because we know what we're doing when it comes to Family Law.

~

Because we'll help you get through the tough times,
not just over them.

~

Because we'll treat you like a person, not a number.

~

Because we'll work on your solutions, not focus on your problems.

~

Because at Woodruff Family Law Group,
you don't get just one of us, you get all of us.

~

When you hire us, you'll have more
than just your attorney—you'll have a united force of talent,
strength, integrity, and experience fighting aggressively
for your best interests.
At Woodruff Family Law Group,
we stand as a TEAM;
there's safety in numbers,
and we look out for our Family.

We are Competency. We are Commitment.
We are Compassion. We are Creativity.
We are TEAM Woodruff Family Law Group.

YOU WILL BE OKAY! YOU WILL SURVIVE THIS! TAKE A DEEP BREATH AND LET'S BEGIN THIS JOURNEY TOGETHER.

CHAPTER EIGHT

TEAM WOODRUFF

TEAM WOODRUFF FAQ

Here are some frequently asked questions. Feel free to reach out to any of us by email or at **336-272-9122** for assistance with your legal matter. **We are taking new clients at this time.**

What are normal business hours?
Our normal business hours are 9:00 AM-5:00 PM Monday through Thursday and 9:00 AM to 2:00 PM on Friday.

When and how can I contact you?
Our switchboard is open 9:00 AM to 5:00 PM on Monday through Thursday and 9:00 AM to 2:00 PM on Friday.

What video chat platforms do you offer for clients?
We are regularly using GoToMeeting, Zoom, Microsoft Teams, and Webex. If you have another program that you would like to use, we will look into using it to accommodate you.

Are you accepting new clients?
Yes. Our initial consult team is in place and working to serve you and your family law needs in this crisis. Call 336-272-9122 and follow the prompts for "initial consult."

You can also visit our website at

Woodruff Family Law Group.
www.woodrufflawfirm.com

Click the "Contact Us" button to complete a contact form, and someone from our team will be in touch with you.

How can I get updates regarding the status of my case or legal matter?
Your best way to get information would be either to call your lead counsel at 336-272-9122 at his/her extension or to email your lead counsel.

Will scheduled depositions, mediation, arbitration, or settlement negotiations occur as planned?
These can occur remotely with video conferencing. Please consult your lead counsel for your options.

For relevant status updates on individual counties and other specific topics, visit us at

Woodruff Family Law Group.
www.woodrufflawfirm.com

Click on the COVID-19 button.

~

TEAM WOODRUFF ATTORNEYS

Our eight attorneys are pictured on the back of this book. Five lawyers at TEAM Woodruff are North Carolina Family Law Specialists. One is also a CPA and a business valuator. Together, we will bring to bear zealous efforts for your legal situation. We only do Family Law.

For more information about each attorney, please go to our website at

Woodruff Family Law Group
www.woodrufflawfirm.com

and click on Our Team.

CHAPTER NINE

WOODRUFF FAMILY LAW GROUP SOCIAL MEDIA, WEBSITE, AND BLOGS

WOODRUFF FAMILY LAW GROUP SOCIAL MEDIA, WEBSITE, & BLOG LINKS

Woodruff Family Law Group ~ Facebook
www.facebook.com/WoodruffFamLaw

Woodruff Family Law Group ~ LinkedIn
www.linkedin.com/company/woodruff-family-law-group/

Carolyn Woodruff ~ LinkedIn
www.linkedin.com/in/carolynwoodruffwoodrufflawfirm/

Woodruff Family Law Group ~ YouTube
www.youtube.com/c/WoodruffLawFirm

Woodruff Family Law Group ~ Twitter
www.twitter.com/woodrufffamlaw

Ask Carolyn ~ Twitter
www.twitter.com/ask_carolyn

Woodruff Family Law Group ~ Instagram
www.instagram.com/woodrufffamlaw/Woodruff

Woodruff Family Law Group ~ Our Website
www.woodrufflawfirm.com

North Carolina Divorce Lawyers Blog
www.northcarolinadivorcelawyersblog.com

Ask Carolyn Woodruff Blog
www.AskCarolynWoodruff.com

Made in the USA
Monee, IL
05 November 2026

67386579R00052